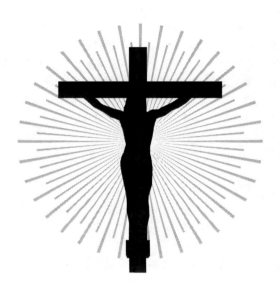

Order of the
HOLY MASS

Introduction

Ever felt a little confused during Mass, not sure what to do or say? Welcome to the Order of the Holy Mass book! This guide is designed to make your experience at Mass more meaningful and enjoyable.

First, we'll learn about the four parts of the Holy Mass: the Introductory Rites, the Liturgy of the Word, the Liturgy of the Eucharist, and Concluding Rites.

Next, we'll go through the order of the Mass, from the priest's words to your responses, so you can join in with confidence.

We'll also explore some special Catholic prayers you can say every day to stay connected with God. Plus, we'll discover the Seven Sacraments, which are special ways we receive God's grace.

Finally, we'll learn the Fruit of the Spirit: love, joy, peace, patience, kindness, goodness, faithfulness, gentleness, and self-control.

Let's get started!

CONTENTS

This is the day the Lord has made.

We will rejoice and be glad in it.
(Psalm 118:24)

PARTS OF THE
HOLY MASS

INTRODUCTORY RITES

We begin each Mass by making the Sign of the Cross. After that, the priest welcomes us to the Mass. Then, we take a moment to think about our sins and ask God for forgiveness. We also sing a happy song to praise God.

THE LITURGY OF THE WORD

It's time to listen and learn from God's Word. We listen to readings from the Bible. These readings, usually from the Old Testament, the Psalms, the New Testament are read out loud by a lector.

The priest or deacon then reads the Gospel and talks to us about these readings, helping us understand and learn from them.

THE LITURGY OF THE EUCHARIST

The Liturgy of the Eucharist is a special moment in Mass when the priest blesses bread and wine, and they transform into Jesus' Body and Blood. Through this sacrament, we remember Jesus' sacrifice for us on the cross so that we could be part of God's family.

CONCLUDING RITES

As our time together comes to an end, we sing thanksgiving songs and say our final prayers. We receive a special blessing from the priest before we go back home, ready to live what we learned.

INTRODUCTORY RITES

Entrance Song

The priest and the servers walk slowly to the altar, while everyone remains standing. Usually an entrance song is sung at this time.

The priest and the servers bow to the altar, and then take their spots. The priest might also go behind the altar and kiss it.

The Sign of the Cross

The Sign of the Cross is how we express our belief in the Holy Trinity—the Father, the Son, and the Holy Spirit.

PRIEST: In the Name of the Father, and of the Son, and of the Holy Spirit.

ALL: Amen

PRIEST: The Lord be with you.

ALL: And with your spirit.

Penitential Act

The Priest calls us to participate in the Penitential Act. It's a time for us to reflect on our sins and humbly ask God for His forgiveness and mercy. We say one of these two prayers:

I confess to almighty God,
and to you, my brothers and sisters,
that I have greatly sinned,
in my thoughts and in my words,
in what I have done and in what I have failed to do,
through my fault, through my fault,
through my most grievous fault;
therefore I ask blessed Mary ever-Virgin,
all the Angels and Saints,
and you, my brothers and sisters,
to pray for me to the Lord our God.

PRIEST: May almighty God have mercy on us, forgive us our sins, and bring us to everlasting life.

ALL: Amen.

OR

PRIEST: You were sent to heal the contrite of heart. Lord, have mercy.

ALL: Lord, have mercy.

PRIEST: You came to call sinners. Christ, have mercy.

ALL: Christ, have mercy.

PRIEST: You are seated at the right hand of the Father to intercede for us. Lord, have mercy.

ALL: Lord, have mercy.

PRIEST: May almighty God have mercy on us, forgive us our sins, and bring us to everlasting life.

ALL: Amen

Gloria

Next, we sing or say the Gloria to praise and honor God. Sometimes we don't sing Gloria, like during Lent.

Glory to God in the highest,
and on earth peace to people of good will.
We praise you, we bless you,
we adore you, we glorify you,
we give you thanks for your great glory,
Lord God, heavenly King,
O God, almighty Father.
Lord Jesus Christ,
Only Begotten Son,
Lord God, Lamb of God, Son of the Father,
you take away the sins of the world,
have mercy on us;
you take away the sins of the world,
receive our prayer;
you are seated at the right hand of the Father,
have mercy on us.
For you alone are the Holy One,
you alone are the Lord,
you alone are the Most High, Jesus Christ,
with the Holy Spirit,
in the glory of God the Father. Amen.

Opening Prayer

PRIEST: Let us pray.
The Priest says a prayer, ending with "We ask this through our Lord Jesus Christ, your Son, who lives and reigns with you and the Holy Spirit, one God for ever and ever. "
OR
Grant this through Christ our Lord.

ALL: Amen

Glory to God in the highest

and on earth peace to people of good will.

THE LITURGY
OF THE WORD

The First Reading

Often read from the Old Testament.

LECTOR: The word of the Lord.
ALL: Thanks be to God.

The Responsorial Psalm

The lector reads from the Book of Psalms, and then everyone joins in by repeating or singing a verse.

The Second Reading

Often read from the New Testament.

LECTOR: The word of the Lord.
ALL: Thanks be to God.

The Gospel Acclamation or Alleluia

We stand up and sing Alleluia! Alleluia! except during Lent.

The Gospel Reading

Read from one of the four Gospels - Luke, Mark, Matthew or John. We remain standing during the Gospel reading.

PRIEST: The Lord be with you.
ALL: And with your spirit.

PRIEST: A reading from the holy Gospel according to...
ALL: Glory to you, O Lord

At the end of the Gospel, the Priest or Deacon says:

PRIEST: The Gospel of the Lord.
ALL: Praise to you, Lord Jesus Christ.

The Homily

We sit back down and listen to the priest or deacon as they preach or talk more about the readings.

The Profession of Faith

We express our beliefs by reciting either the Apostle's Creed or the Nicene Creed.

Nicene Creed

I believe in one God,
the Father almighty,
maker of heaven and earth,
of all things visible and invisible.

I believe in one Lord Jesus Christ,
the Only Begotten Son of God,
born of the Father before all ages.
God from God, Light from Light,
true God from true God,
begotten, not made, consubstantial with the Father;
through him all things were made.
For us men and for our salvation he came down from heaven,
and by the Holy Spirit was incarnate of the Virgin Mary,
and became man.

For our sake he was crucified under Pontius Pilate,
he suffered death and was buried,
and rose again on the third day
in accordance with the Scriptures.
He ascended into heaven
and is seated at the right hand of the Father.
He will come again in glory
to judge the living and the dead
and his kingdom will have no end.

I believe in the Holy Spirit, the Lord, the giver of life,
who proceeds from the Father and the Son,
who with the Father and the Son is adored and glorified,

who has spoken through the prophets.

I believe in one, holy, Catholic and apostolic Church.
I confess one Baptism for the forgiveness of sins
and I look forward to the resurrection of the dead
and the life of the world to come. Amen.

The Apostles' Creed

I believe in God,
the Father almighty,
Creator of heaven and earth,
and in Jesus Christ, his only Son, our Lord,
who was conceived by the Holy Spirit,
born of the Virgin Mary,
suffered under Pontius Pilate,
was crucified, died and was buried;
he descended into hell;
on the third day he rose again from the dead;
he ascended into heaven,
and is seated at the right hand of God the Father
almighty;
from there he will come to judge the living and the dead.

I believe in the Holy Spirit,
the holy Catholic Church,
the communion of saints,
the forgiveness of sins,
the resurrection of the body,
and life everlasting. Amen.

The Prayer of the Faithful

We pray for our needs, the needs of others, for our
church, our community, and the world.

PETITIONER: We pray to the Lord
ALL: Lord, hear our prayer.

THE LITURGY OF THE EUCHARIST

This is my body given for you;
do this in remembrance of me.
(Luke 22:19b)

The Offertory

The Liturgy of the Eucharist kicks off with the offertory. During the Offertory Song the gifts of bread and wine are brought to the altar in a procession. We might also bring other gifts to help support the Church and those in need.

The Priest offers a prayer of blessing quietly at the altar. Sometimes these prayers are said aloud and each time we answer:

Blessed be God for ever.

PRIEST: Pray, brothers and sisters, that my sacrifice and yours may be acceptable to God, the almighty Father

ALL: May the Lord accept the sacrifice at your hands for the praise and glory of his name, for our good and the good of all his holy Church.

The Eucharistic Prayer (Preface)

PRIEST: The Lord be with you.
ALL: And with your spirit.

PRIEST: Lift up your hearts.
ALL: We lift them up to the Lord.

PRIEST: Let us give thanks to the Lord our God.
ALL: It is right and just.

This next part is very special. This is where the bread and wine get changed into the Body and Blood of Christ. The priest says a prayer, then everyone sings or says the Sanctus together.

The Sanctus

Holy, Holy, Holy Lord God of hosts
Heaven and earth are full of your glory
Hosanna in the highest
Blessed is he who comes in the name of the Lord
Hosanna in the highest.

We kneel for the rest of the Eucharistic Prayer.

The Eucharistic Prayer (Continued)

The Priest reminds us of the Last Supper. Holding up the bread, the priest says the words Jesus said:

Take this, all of you, and eat it:
This is my body which will be given up for you.

As these words are said, the bread changes into the Body of Christ. This is such a special moment that bells are sometimes rung.

As the priest shows the Body of Christ to you, you can quietly pray, "My Lord, and my God." After this, you should bow your head, as the priest genuflects.

The priest says more prayers, holds up the cup of wine, and says the words Jesus said:

Take this, all of you, and drink from it:
This is the cup of my blood,
The blood of the new and everlasting covenant.
It will be shed for you and for all
So that sins may be forgiven.
Do this in memory of me.

As these words are said, the wine changes into the Blood of Christ. Again, bells might be rung.

As the priest show the cup with the Blood of Christ to you, you can quietly pray, "My Lord, and my God." After this, you should bow your head, as the priest genuflects.

The Mystery of Faith.

PRIEST: The mystery of faith.

ALL: We proclaim your Death, O Lord,
and profess your Resurrection
until you come again.

OR

When we eat this bread and drink this cup,
we proclaim your death, O Lord,
until you come again.

OR

Save us, Saviour of the world,
for by your cross and Resurrection
you have set us free.

The Priest then takes the chalice and the paten with the host and, raising both, he alone says:

**Through him, and with him, and in him,
O God, almighty Father,
in the unity of the Holy Spirit,
all glory and honor is yours,
for ever and ever.**

ALL: Amen

The Lord's Prayer

PRIEST: At the Savior's command and formed by
divine teaching, we dare to say:

ALL: Our Father, who art in heaven,
hallowed be thy name;
thy kingdom come,
thy will be done
on earth as it is in heaven.
Give us this day our daily bread,
and forgive us our trespasses,
as we forgive those who trespass against us;
and lead us not into temptation,
but deliver us from evil.

PRIEST: Deliver us, Lord, we pray, from every evil,
graciously grant peace in our days,
that, by the help of your mercy,
we may be always free from sin
and safe from all distress,
as we await the blessed hope
and the coming of our Saviour, Jesus Christ.

ALL: For the kingdom, the power and the glory
are yours now and for ever.

The Sign of Peace

PRIEST: Lord Jesus Christ,
who said to your Apostles:
Peace I leave you, my peace I give you,
look not on our sins,
but on the faith of your Church,
and graciously grant her peace and unity
in accordance with your will.
Who live and reign for ever and ever.

ALL: Amen

PRIEST: The peace of the Lord be with you always.

ALL: And with your spirit.

PRIEST: Let us offer each other the sign of peace.

It's now time to give the sign of peace. We may shake hands with the people around us, and say to them, "Peace be with you".

Breaking of the Bread

Lamb of God, you take away the sins of the world,
   have mercy on us.
Lamb of God, you take away the sins of the world,
   have mercy on us.
Lamb of God, you take away the sins of the world,
   grant us peace.

Invitation to Communion

PRIEST: Behold the Lamb of God, behold him who takes away the sins of the world.
Blessed are those called to the supper of the Lamb.

ALL: Lord, I am not worthy that you should enter under my roof, but only say the word and my soul shall be healed.

Prayer after Communion

PRIEST: Let us pray.

All stand and pray in silence. Then the Priest says the Prayer after Communion, at the end of which we say Amen.

Concluding Rites

Blessing

PRIEST: The Lord be with you.
ALL: And with your spirit.
PRIEST: May almighty God bless you, the Father, and the Son, and the Holy Spirit ✠
ALL: Amen

Dismissal

PRIEST: Go forth, the Mass is ended.
Or: Go and announce the Gospel of the Lord.
Or: Go in peace, glorifying the Lord by your life.
Or: Go in peace.

ALL: Thanks be to God.

CATHOLIC DAILY
PRAYERS

Do not be anxious about anything,

but in every situation, by prayer and petition, with thanksgiving, present your requests to God. And the peace of God, which transcends all understanding, will guard your hearts and your minds in Christ Jesus. (Philippians 4:6-7)

The Lords Prayer

Our Father, who art in heaven,
hallowed be Thy name.
Thy kingdom come;
Thy will be done on earth as it is in heaven.
Give us this day our daily bread;
and forgive us our trespasses
as we forgive those who trespass against us;
and lead us not into temptation,
but deliver us from evil.
Amen.

Hail Mary

Hail Mary, Full of Grace,
The Lord is with thee.
Blessed art thou among women,
and blessed is the fruit of thy womb, Jesus.
Holy Mary, Mother of God, pray for us sinners
now, and at the hour of our death.
Amen.

Glory Be

Glory be to the Father,
and to the Son,
and to the Holy Spirit.
As it was in the beginning, is now, and ever shall be,
world without end.
Amen.

Prayer To Your Guardian Angel

Angel of God, my guardian dear,
To whom God's love commits me here,
Ever this day, be at my side,
To light and guard, Rule and guide.
Amen.

Prayer to the Holy Spirit.

Come, Holy Spirit, fill the hearts of your faithful and kindle in them the fire of your love.
Send forth your Spirit and they shall be created, and you shall renew the face of the earth.

Let us pray.

O God, who have taught the hearts of the faithful by the light of the Holy Spirit, grant that in the same Spirit we may be truly wise and ever rejoice in his consolation.
Through Christ our Lord. Amen.

Act of Contrition

My God, I am sorry for my sins with all my heart.
In choosing to do wrong and failing to do good,
I have sinned against you
whom I should love above all things.
I firmly intend, with your help, to do penance,
to sin no more,
and to avoid whatever leads me to sin.
Our Savior Jesus Christ suffered and died for us.
In His name. My God have mercy.
Amen

Grace before meals

Bless us, Oh Lord,
and these thy gifts,
which we are about to receive,
from thy bounty,
through Christ, Our Lord. Amen

Grace after meals

We give Thee thanks for all Thy benefits,
O Almighty God, who lives and reigns for ever;
and may the souls of the faithful departed,
through the mercy of God, rest in peace. Amen.

Act of Love

O Lord God,
I love you above all things and I love my neighbor for
your sake because you are the highest, infinite and
perfect good, worthy of all my love.
In this love I intend to live and die. Amen.

Act of Hope

O Lord God,
I hope by your grace for the pardon of all my sins and
after life here to gain eternal happiness because you
have promised it who are infinitely powerful, faithful,
kind, and merciful.
In this hope I intend to live and die. Amen.

Act of Charity

O my God, I love You above all things,
with my whole heart and soul,
because You are all-good and worthy of all love.
I love my neighbor as myself for the love of You.
I forgive all who have injured me,
and ask pardon of all whom I have injured. Amen.

Prayer to St. Michael

St. Michael The Archangel,
defend us in the day of battle;
be our safeguard against the wickedness and snares of
the devil.
May God rebuke him, we humbly pray,
and do thou, O Prince of the heavenly host,
by the power of God,
cast into hell, satan and all the other evil spirits,
who prowl through the world, seeking the ruin of souls.
Amen.

Soul of Christ

Soul of Christ, sanctify me.
Body of Christ, save me.
Blood of Christ, inebriate me.
Water from the side of Christ, wash me.
Passion of Christ, strengthen me.
O Good Jesus, hear me.
Within Thy wounds hide me.
Suffer me not to be separated from thee.
From the malignant enemy defend me.
In the hour of my death call me.
And bid me come unto Thee,
That with all Thy saints,
I may praise thee Forever and ever. Amen.

THE SEVEN SACRAMENTS

OF THE CATHOLIC CHURCH

THE SEVEN SACRAMENTS

Sacraments are special signs and celebrations that Jesus gave his Church. These sacraments allow us to share in God's life and work. They help us grow closer to Jesus and each other by helping us become more like Him.

✓ **BAPTISM**

✓ **EUCHARIST**

✓ **CONFIRMATION**

✓ **RECONCILIATION**

✓ **HOLY ORDERS**

✓ **MATRIMONY**

✓ **ANOINTING OF THE SICK**

THE SACRAMENT OF BAPTISM

Baptism is a sacrament where we are made children of God and become members of the Church.

The Forgiveness of Sins

Through Baptism, we receive forgiveness for all our sins, including the original sin committed by Adam and Eve, and any sins we have committed ourselves

The Baptism Ceremony

During the ceremony, the priest pours water over the person's head and says, "I now baptize you in the name of the Father, and of the Son, and of the Holy Ghost."

The Symbols of Baptism

The symbols of Baptism are water, a white garment, oil, and light (a candle).

Water represents cleansing from sin and the rebirth into a new life in Christ. The priest also drapes a white cloth over the baptized, symbolizing purity and new life.

The baptismal candle symbolizes the light of Christ and signifies that Christ has come into the baptized's life.

THE EUCHARIST

Each time we celebrate the Eucharist, we remember Jesus' death and resurrection.

The Eucharist is a powerful symbol of God's love for us. Through this sacrament, we remember Jesus' sacrifice on the cross so that we can be part of God's family.

The Holy Eucharist feeds us and strengthens us, helping us become the people God created us to be.

The Symbols of the Holy Eucharist

The symbols of the Holy Eucharist are the bread and wine, which become the Body and Blood of Christ when they're blessed by a priest during Mass.

CONFIRMATION

CONFIRMATION IS A SACRAMENT BY WHICH WE RECEIVE THE HOLY SPIRIT, IN ORDER TO MAKE US STRONG AND PERFECT CHRISTIANS AND SOLDIERS OF JESUS CHRIST.

In the Sacrament of Confirmation, the baptized person is "sealed with the gift of the Holy Spirit" and is strengthened for service to the Body of Christ.

During Confirmation, God gives us more grace and more gifts through His Holy Spirit, so we can do the work God created us to do.

Sometimes Confirmation is shown as Tongues of Fire, signifying the power of the Holy Spirit coming onto the person being confirmed.

The bishop dips his right thumb in the chrism and makes the sign of the cross on the forehead of the one to be confirmed, as he says: *"(Name), be sealed with the gift of the Holy Spirit"*. The newly confirmed responds: *Amen.*

RECONCILIATION

In the sacrament of Reconciliation, we confess our sins to God and ask for His forgiveness.

Every time we sin, we hurt ourselves, other people and God.

In Reconciliation, we acknowledge our sins before God and the Church. We do this in a special rite called Confession or Penance. During confession, we talk to a priest and tell him what we did wrong.

The priest helps us say sorry to God and gives us a special blessing and instructions.

The Absolution

The priest says:
'I absolve you from your sins, in the name of the Father, and of the Son, and of the Holy Spirit'.

This blessing is called absolution. It means that God has forgiven us and that we can start fresh and try to do better.

No matter what we've done wrong, God will forgive us if we are truly sorry and ask for forgiveness.

THE ANOINTING OF THE SICK

This sacrament is given to a person who is seriously ill or near death.

Who administers this Sacrament?

The Sacrament of Anointing of the Sick is given by a priest. He blesses the sick person with holy oil and prays with them for healing and spiritual strength.

The special grace of this sacrament gives sick person the courage to face their illness, just like Jesus suffered on the Cross for us.

Forgiveness of sins.

The Sacrament of Anointing of the Sick also brings forgiveness of sins. Sometimes, when a person is very sick, they may not be able to go to Confession.

But through the Sacrament of the Anointing of the Sick, they can receive forgiveness and know that God loves them and forgives them.

MATRIMONY

Matrimony is the Sacrament which sanctifies the contract of a Christian marriage. This means that the joining together of a man and a woman is blessed and made holy and pleasing to God.

The couple promises to love and honor each other all the days of their lives. They vow to take care of each other and the children with which they are blessed. They also promise to be faithful to each other.

When a man and a woman get married, they receive a special grace from God. This gift helps them to love each other, be faithful, and raise their children to know and love God.

During the wedding, the couple exchanges special rings to show that they belong to each other. This is a symbol of their love and commitment to one another.

HOLY ORDERS

Holy Orders is the Sacrament by which bishops, priests, and deacons of the Church are ordained, and receive power and grace to perform their sacred duties.

A vocation

Taking Holy Orders is a big commitment. Yet it is a great way for us to serve God and our community.

Those who are called to this vocation spend many years preparing for it. They study theology, learn about the teachings of the Church, and develop their spiritual life through prayer and reflection.

The Ceremony

During the ordination ceremony, the bishop lays his hands on them, anoints them with oil, and says a special prayer:

'Grant, we implore Thee. Almighty Father, to this Thy servant the dignity of the Priesthood (for priests)".

Duties

Once ordained, priests, deacons, and bishops become important leaders in their communities. They have special roles, like saying the Mass and administering Sacraments.

They provide spiritual guidance and support to others. They also share the teachings of the Church and help people grow in their faith.

Fruit of the spirit

But the fruit of the Spirit is love, joy, peace, patience, kindness, goodness, faithfulness, gentleness, self-control; against such things there no law.

Galatians 5:22-23

FRUIT OF THE SPIRIT

COLOR THE FRUITS OF THE SPIRIT

LOVE

PEACE

SELF-CONTROL

PATIENCE

GOODNESS

KINDNESS

FAITHFULNESS

JOY

GENTLENESS

Made in United States
Cleveland, OH
11 May 2025

16848543R00026